FINANCE

Exploring Career Pathways

Diane Lindsey Reeves

Created and produced by
Bright Futures Press, Cary, North Carolina
www.brightfuturespress.com

Published by
Cherry Lake Publishing, Ann Arbor, Michigan
www.cherrylakepublishing.com

Photo Credits: Cover, Beautyline; page 7, SFIO CRACHO, ST22Studio, Monkey Business Images, SP Photo, Dmitry Kalinovsky, Andy Dean Photography, TZIDOSUN, Isak55; page 8, SFIO CRACHO; page 10, ST22Studio; page 12, Monkey Business Images; page 14, SP Photo; page 16, Dmitry Kalinovsky; page 18, Andy Dean Photography; page 20, TZIDOSUN; page 22, Isak 55; page 24, Number1411.

Library of Congress Cataloging-in-Publication Date

CIP data has been filed and is available at catalog.loc.gov.

Printed in the United States of America.

TABLE OF CONTENTS

HELLO WORLD OF WORK

This is you.

Right now, your job is to go to school and learn all you can.

This is the world of work.

It's where people earn a living, find purpose in their lives, and make the world a better place.

Sooner or later, you'll have to find your way from

HERE to THERE.

To get started, take all the jobs in the incredibly enormous world of work and organize them into an imaginary pile. It's a big pile, isn't it? It would be pretty tricky to find the perfect job for you among so many options.

No worries!

Some very smart career experts have made it easier to figure out. They sorted jobs and industries into groups by the types of skills and products they share. These groups are called career clusters. They provide pathways that will make it easier for you to find career options that match your interests.

 Architecture & Construction

Arts & Communication

 Business & Administration

Education & Training

 Finance

Food & Natural Resources

 Government

Health Sciences

Hospitality & Tourism

Human Services

Information Technology

Law & Public Safety

Manufacturing

Marketing, Sales & Service

Science, Technology, Engineering & Mathematics (STEM)

Transportation

Good thing you are still a kid.

You have lots of time to explore ideas and imagine yourself doing all kinds of amazing things. The **World of Work** (WoW for short) series of books will help you get started.

TAKE A HIKE!

There are 16 career pathways waiting for you to explore. The only question is: Which one should you explore first?

Is **Finance** a good path for you to start exploring career ideas? There is a lot to like about this pathway. These professionals keep track of money for people, businesses, and governments. They work in accounting, banking, business, insurance, and investing.

See if any of the following questions grab your interest.

WOULD YOU ENJOY earning and saving money, being the class treasurer, or playing the stock market game?

CAN YOU IMAGINE someday working at an accounting firm, bank, or Wall Street stock exchange?

ARE YOU CURIOUS ABOUT what accountants, bankers, fraud investigators, property managers, or stockbrokers do?

If so, it's time to take a hike! Keep reading to see what kinds of opportunities you can discover along the Finance pathway.

But wait!

What if you don't think you'll like this pathway?

You have two choices.

You could keep reading, to find out more than you already know. You might be surprised to learn how many amazing careers you'll find along this path.

OR

Turn to page 27 to get ideas about other WoW pathways.

MORTGAGE BROKER

CHIEF FINANCIAL OFFICER

PURCHASING AGENT

INSURANCE CLAIMS AGENT

WoW Up Close

Buy and sell stocks on Wall Street. Protect people's homes, health, and possessions with insurance. Keep tabs on the money that businesses earn and spend. Take care of the world's banking needs. These are just some of the important jobs that people who work along the Finance pathway do.

FORENSIC ACCOUNTANT

ACTUARY

FINANCIAL PLANNER

STOCKBROKER

ACTUARY

An **actuary** has one of those jobs that most people never hear about. And the job name itself sure doesn't give you any clues as to what this worker does!

Have you ever heard of **risk**? An actuary uses math to calculate how likely it is that something bad will happen in the future.

For example, how likely is it that this book is going to fly out the window and trip someone walking down the street? An actuary would say probably not very likely. But if you left this book on a park bench, is it likely someone would steal it? Maybe so, which would lead an actuary to analyze the risk.

Actuaries work with risks. Their job is to determine how likely it is for something bad to happen to someone's health, their property, or their business. Then they figure out how much it would cost if something bad did happen. What they discover helps companies figure how much to charge for insurance premiums and other protections.

Actuaries work with lots of data and lots of numbers. They mostly work for **insurance** companies, but big companies, government agencies, and accounting firms have actuaries on staff, too. Wherever they work, their job is to analyze the data and crunch the numbers to find answers to complex problems.

Check It Out!

Play around with some math skills at

▶ http://www.mathgames.com

▶ http://www.mathplayground.com

▶ http://www.coolmath-games.com

Start Now!

✔ See what it is like to be an actuary at http://www.beanactuary.org.

✔ Ask a teacher or parent to help you compete in an online math challenge at http://www.mathbuddyonline.com/mathlathon.

CHIEF FINANCIAL OFFICER

Job titles that include the word chief are usually high-powered and high-paying. That certainly tends to be the case with a **chief financial officer**. This person typically works for a big company and is one of the company's top **executives**.

The main job of a chief financial officer, or CFO, is to manage a company's money. CFOs are in charge of a company's accounting, finance, and investment activities. They analyze financial data to find out where the company is doing well and identify areas where there might be problems. This information helps the company make decisions about which products and services to offer and how to make the company more profitable.

No one is hired as a CFO right out of college. You need lots of experience and top-notch skills to reach the executive suite. CFOs often get started with a college degree in finance or accounting. Then they go on to earn a **master of business administration** (MBA) and spend several years climbing the corporate ladder. Once they earn the top financial spot in a company, they get the chance to be a real influence on the success of the company.

Check It Out!

Find links to kid-friendly Web sites about money at

➤ https://kids.usa.gov/money

Start Now!

- Run for treasurer of your student government or favorite after-school club.

- Make a budget for using your allowance to save, spend, and give.

- Talk with your parents about ways to help your family save money.

FINANCIAL PLANNER

Most people work hard for their money. When they have extra money to save, they want to find ways to put that money to work making more money. They need **investments**. They need to figure out legal ways to save money on taxes.

They need to make sure they have the best types of insurance to protect their families. That's when they turn to **financial planners** for advice.

Not just anyone can offer financial advice. Financial planners must be certified. Getting certified involves four Es. A solid education is the first E. Financial planners must have at least a college **degree** in a field like finance or business. They must get thousands of hours of experience (the second E) working under a qualified supervisor. Then they must pass a special exam (the third E). After all that, they must follow strict rules about **ethics** (the final E). This means they must have a clean record with no history of criminal or financial problems.

Besides having financial know-how, financial planners must be trustworthy. The money people invest is often needed for things like their children's education and their own retirement. It's not about getting rich—it's part of securing their financial future. People depend on financial planners to give good advice and to take good care of their money.

Check It Out!

Finding ideas for making and saving money at

▶ http://www.themint.org/kids

▶ http://bit.ly/SavingsRoadTrip

Start Now!

✔ Set up a savings account at a local bank and watch your money grow as you make regular deposits.

✔ Make a plan for buying something really cool, like a bike, smartphone, or video game. Figure out how much you need to earn and save, and for how long, to make it possible.

FORENSIC ACCOUNTANT

Follow the money! **Forensic accountants** follow this advice to crack criminal cases involving money. They use numbers to find wrongdoing like **embezzlement**, **fraud**, and **money laundering**. They look through financial statements, **spreadsheets**, and other records to find clues proving that the numbers do not add up.

The types of crimes that forensic accountants investigate are called **white-collar crimes**. For the most part, there is no blood-and-guts involved—no one gets physically hurt. But financial crimes can cause great damage to individuals, businesses, and governments.

Forensic accountants have to be curious and creative. Curiosity keeps them hunting for evidence in page after page of records. Being creative helps them figure out how people try to cover their tracks and hide their bad behavior.

They also need good training. A college degree in accounting or finance is required. More education in criminal justice or law enforcement helps.

Forensic accountants work wherever investigative accounting is needed. This obviously includes private accounting firms and police departments. But did you know that the **FBI** has a whole division of special agents who work on white-collar crimes? It even has a "most wanted" criminal list!

Check It Out!

Investigate famous white-collar crime cases at

▶ http://bit.ly/WhiteCollar1

▶ http://bit.ly/WhiteCollar2

Start Now!

✔ Read a good mystery story and try to figure out whodunit!

✔ Try cracking some online cases at http://kids.mysterynet.com.

✔ Explore what it's like to be an FBI special agent at http://bit.ly/FBIAgentKids.

INSURANCE CLAIMS AGENT

Fast-forward a few years and imagine that you have your driver's license and just bought your first car. Then along comes a big storm that knocks a heavy tree branch down on top of your car. Squish! Good thing you have car insurance. Help is just a phone call away.

You call your insurance company and tell your story to an **insurance claims agent**. This person takes down all the information and explains what you need to do to get the car fixed. You (or, more likely, your parents!) will probably have to pay a **deductible**. But that will be a lot cheaper than buying a new car. Before long, you are back behind the wheel, safely driving yourself around town.

Car insurance is just one type of insurance that claims agents specialize in. Other types are home, health, property, or life insurance. Their job is to determine what each customer's insurance policy covers and to get that person as much help as possible.

Claims agents handle many claims at once, so they have to be very organized. They tend to use special computer programs to keep track of all the paperwork. They must also be courteous and able to deal with customers who may be having one of the worst days of their lives. This would certainly be true for someone whose home has been destroyed in a fire or hurricane. In those types of situations, having insurance can be a real life-saver!

Check It Out!

Learn about insurance at

▶ http://playinsure.com

▶ http://www.tdi.texas.gov/kids/index.html

Start Now!

✔ Ask your parents about the different kinds of insurance your family has.

✔ Go online and explore the website of the insurance company your family uses.

✔ Check out some unbelievable but true insurance claims at https://www.farmers.com/hall-of-claims.

MORTGAGE BROKER

For most people, a house is the most expensive thing they will ever buy—by a long shot! In fact, homes are so expensive that most people don't have enough cash to buy them outright. They need to get a loan. A loan used to buy a house is called a **mortgage**.

Mortgage brokers help people buying houses get mortgages. Since there is so much money involved, these types of loans are complicated. Mortgage brokers have to check into the buyer's financial history to make sure that the person has the ability to pay back the loan. They look at how much money the borrower makes and how much money is owed for other things like car loans. They also check to see if the person has a good history of paying bills on time. The home the person wants to buy must get an **appraisal** so the bank knows that it is actually worth the loan amount.

As you can imagine, there is lots of paperwork involved in all of this. It's the mortgage broker's job to make sure every T is crossed and every I is dotted—that means absolutely everything must be in perfect order. So mortgage brokers have to be very organized and be able to use technology to gather information. They must also be good at working with people and explaining complicated things.

You don't need a college degree to become a mortgage broker. However, you do need special training and must pass a licensing exam.

Check It Out!

Go online and watch episodes of real estate shows like *Fixer Upper* and *Love It or List It*.

▶ http://www.hgtv.com

Start Now!

- ✔ Draw a picture and describe the type of house you hope to buy someday.

- ✔ Imagine you have a customer who wants to buy a house for $250,000. Go online to http://www.mortgagecalculator.org to find out how much the monthly payment would be with 4 percent interest over 20 years.

PURCHASING AGENT

Chances are that someone, probably a parent, takes care of buying the food, clothes, and other necessities that your family uses. This person doesn't have an official job title and doesn't get paid for doing these tasks. But tracking down products with good value at a good price is exactly what **purchasing agents** do.

Of course, purchasing agents have **budgets** that are quite a bit larger than the one a typical family has. Agents must buy supplies for an entire company. For instance, think of your favorite potato chip brand. Purchasing agents for that company have to buy enough potatoes, oil, salt, and packaging materials to keep millions of people enjoying their favorite crunchy snacks.

Purchasing agents become experts at the types of products they have to buy. After all, not just any potato will do when it comes to making chips. They build relationships with **vendors** who provide quality products and reliable service. They use special computer software to keep track of every purchase they make. They must also make sure that deliveries are made and bills are paid on time.

If ever there was an ideal career for a "shop till you drop" type of person, a purchasing agent is it!

Check It Out!

Go online to visit the Web sites of some of your favorite brands. Try to imagine the types of supplies a purchasing agent would need to buy for each company.

Start Now!

- ✔ Clip grocery coupons from the local Sunday paper to help your family's "purchasing agent" get the best deals on food.

- ✔ The next time you need a new pair of jeans (or some other fashion item), go online to compare prices at several different stores.

- ✔ Make a list of at least five ways that purchasing agents use math to do their jobs.

STOCKBROKER

Let's say you own a big, successful company. You need money to create new products or hire lots of employees. Where can you get the kind of cash it takes to move your company to the big time?

One way is to sell **stock** in your company on the **stock exchange**.

The stock exchange is where people invest their money in promising companies. They buy stocks or bonds with the hope that the company will become even more successful. When it does, **stockholders** sell their stocks and bonds for more than they paid for them.

For instance, Amazon (a huge online retailer) originally offered its stock for $18 per share in 1997. By 2016, that same stock cost around $760 per share. That's an increase in value of almost 48,000 percent! if you were lucky enough to buy $3,000 worth of Amazon stock back then, it would have been worth $1 million by 2016!

Not all stocks are quite that successful, but it is up to **stockbrokers** to help investors buy and sell stocks. They do this through stock exchanges located in places like Wall Street in New York City. Computers now make it possible to buy and sell stocks in a fraction of a second from anyplace in the world. It takes lots of research and skill—and lots of special training—to identify winning stocks and help investors make smart investments.

Check It Out!

Find out how the stock market works at

▶ http://bit.ly/StockMarketA

▶ http://bit.ly/StockMarketB

▶ http://bit.ly/StockMarketC

Start Now!

✔ Ask a parent or teacher to help you play the Stock Market Game at http://www.smgww.org.

✔ Go online to http://finance.yahoo.com to see how the stock for your favorite fast food or clothing brand is doing. Simply type the name of the company in the search bar.

Abstractor • Account executive • Account representative • Actuarial analyst • **ACTUARY** • Administrative assistant • Appraiser • Banker • Banking center manager • Bank teller • Bill collector • Branch manager • Broker • Budget analyst • Business manager • Business teacher • Certified fraud examiner • Certified income tax preparer • **CHIEF FINANCIAL OFFICER** • Chief risk officer • Claims representative • Claims agent • Claims examiner • Client manager • Closer • Collections manager • Commercial title examiner • Commodities banker • Commodities broker • Commodities loan officer • Comptroller • Corporate bond trader •

WoW Big List

Take a look at some of the different kinds of jobs people do in the Finance pathway. **WoW!**

Some of these job titles will be familiar to you. Others will be so unfamiliar that you will scratch your head and say "huh?"

Credit clerk • Credit manager • Customer care specialist • Customer relationship specialist • Customer service representative • Energy broker • Equity analyst • Equity trader • Field inspector • Finance director • Financial advisor • Financial aid officer • Financial analyst • Financial assistance advisor • **FINANCIAL PLANNER** • Financial qualitative analyst • **FORENSIC ACCOUNTANT** • Global risk management director • Health actuary • Inspector general • Insurance appraiser • Insurance broker • Insurance claims investigator • **INSURANCE CLAIMS AGENT** • Insurance sales agent • Investment analyst • Investment director • Investment trader • Litigation claim representative • Loan counselor • Loan processor • **MORTGAGE BROKER** • Mortgage loan originator • New accounts representative • Operations clerk • Options trader • Patient account representative • Personal banker • Planning analyst • Portfolio manager • Pricing actuary • Product development actuary • **PURCHASING AGENT** • Real estate analyst • Regional manager • Relationship manager • Retail

Find a job title that makes you curious. Type the name of the job into your favorite Internet search engine and find out more about the people who have that job.

1 What do they do?

2 Where do they work?

3 How much training do they need to do this job?

banker • Risk analyst • Risk and insurance consultant • Risk management specialist • Risk manager • Sales director • Sales representative • Sales trader • Securities analyst • Securities lending trader • Select banker • Service center manager • Special agent • **STOCKBROKER** • Tax consultant • Tax preparer • Telemarketer • Teller coordinator • Title searcher • Trader • Trading assistant • Treasurer • Trust officer • Underwriter

TAKE YOUR PICK

	Put stars next to your 3 favorite career ideas	Put an X next to the career idea you like the least	Put a question mark next to the career idea you want to learn more about
Actuary			
Chief financial officer			
Financial planner			
Forensic accountant			
Insurance claims agent			
Mortgage broker			
Purchasing agent			
Stockbroker			
	What do you like most about these careers?	What is it about this career that doesn't appeal to you?	What do you want to learn about this career? Where can you find answers?

Which Big Wow List ideas are you curious about?

EXPLORE SOME MORE

The Finance pathway is only one of 16 career pathways that hold exciting options for your future. Take a look at the other 15 to figure out where to start exploring next.

 ## Architecture & Construction

WOULD YOU ENJOY making things with LEGOs™, building a treehouse or birdhouse, or designing the world's best skate park?

CAN YOU IMAGINE someday working at a construction site, a design firm, or a building company?

ARE YOU CURIOUS ABOUT what civil engineers, demolition technicians, heavy-equipment operators, landscape architects, or urban planners do?

 ## Arts & Communication

WOULD YOU ENJOY drawing your own cartoons, using your smartphone to make a movie, or writing articles for the student newspaper?

CAN YOU IMAGINE someday working at a Hollywood movie studio, a publishing company, or a television news station?

ARE YOU CURIOUS ABOUT what actors, bloggers, graphic designers, museum curators, or writers do?

 ## Business & Administration

WOULD YOU ENJOY playing Monopoly, being the boss of your favorite club or team, or starting your own business?

CAN YOU IMAGINE someday working at a big corporate headquarters, government agency, or international business center?

ARE YOU CURIOUS ABOUT what brand managers, chief executive officers, e-commerce analysts, entrepreneurs, or purchasing agents do?

 ## Education & Training

WOULD YOU ENJOY babysitting, teaching your grandparents how to use a computer, or running a summer camp for neighbor kids in your backyard?

CAN YOU IMAGINE someday working at a college counseling center, corporate training center, or school?

ARE YOU CURIOUS ABOUT what animal trainers, coaches, college professors, guidance counselors, or principals do?

Food & Natural Resources

WOULD YOU ENJOY exploring nature, growing your own garden, or setting up a recycling center at your school?

CAN YOU IMAGINE someday working at a national park, raising crops in a city farm, or studying food in a laboratory?

ARE YOU CURIOUS ABOUT what landscape architects, chefs, food scientists, environmental engineers, or forest rangers do?

 ## Government

WOULD YOU ENJOY reading about U.S. presidents, running for student council, or helping a favorite candidate win an election?

CAN YOU IMAGINE someday working at a chamber of commerce, government agency, or law firm?

ARE YOU CURIOUS about what mayors, customs agents, federal special agents, intelligence analysts, or politicians do?

 ## Health Sciences

WOULD YOU ENJOY nursing a sick pet back to health, dissecting animals in a science lab, or helping the school coach run a sports clinic?

CAN YOU IMAGINE someday working at a dental office, hospital, or veterinary clinic?

ARE YOU CURIOUS ABOUT what art therapists, doctors, dentists, pharmacists, and veterinarians do?

 ## Hospitality & Tourism

WOULD YOU ENJOY traveling, sightseeing, or meeting people from other countries?

CAN YOU IMAGINE someday working at a convention center, resort, or travel agency?

ARE YOU CURIOUS ABOUT what convention planners, golf pros, tour guides, resort managers, or wedding planners do?

 ## Human Services

WOULD YOU ENJOY showing a new kid around your school, organizing a neighborhood food drive, or being a peer mediator?

CAN YOU IMAGINE someday working at an elder care center, fitness center, or mental health center?

ARE YOU CURIOUS ABOUT what elder care center directors, hairstylists, personal trainers, psychologists, or religious leaders do?

 ## Information Technology

WOULD YOU ENJOY creating your own video game, setting up a Web site, or building your own computer?

CAN YOU IMAGINE someday working at an information technology start-up company, software design firm, or research and development laboratory?

ARE YOU CURIOUS ABOUT what artificial intelligence scientists, big data analysts, computer forensic investigators, software engineers, or video game designers do?

Law & Public Safety

WOULD YOU ENJOY working on the school safety patrol, participating in a mock court trial at school, or coming up with a fire escape plan for your home?

CAN YOU IMAGINE someday working at a cyber security company, fire station, police department, or prison?

ARE YOU CURIOUS ABOUT what animal control officers, coroners, detectives, firefighters, or park rangers do?

Manufacturing

WOULD YOU ENJOY figuring out how things are made, competing in a robot-building contest, or putting model airplanes together?

CAN YOU IMAGINE someday working at a high-tech manufacturing plant, engineering firm, or global logistics company?

ARE YOU CURIOUS ABOUT what chemical engineers, industrial designers, supply chain managers, robotics technologists, or welders do?

Marketing, Sales & Service

WOULD YOU ENJOY keeping up with the latest fashion trends, picking favorite TV commercials during Super Bowl games, or making posters for a favorite school club?

CAN YOU IMAGINE someday working at an advertising agency, corporate marketing department, or retail store?

ARE YOU CURIOUS ABOUT what creative directors, market researchers, media buyers, retail store managers, and social media consultants do?

Science, Technology, Engineering & Mathematics (STEM)

WOULD YOU ENJOY concocting experiments in a science lab, trying out the latest smartphone, or taking advanced math classes?

CAN YOU IMAGINE someday working in a science laboratory, engineering firm, or research and development center?

ARE YOU CURIOUS ABOUT what aeronautical engineers, ecologists, statisticians, oceanographers, or zoologists do?

Transportation

WOULD YOU ENJOY taking pilot or sailing lessons, watching a NASA rocket launch, or helping out in the school carpool lane?

CAN YOU IMAGINE someday working at an airport, mass transit system, or shipping port?

ARE YOU CURIOUS ABOUT what air traffic controllers, flight attendants, logistics planners, surveyors, and traffic engineers do?

MY WoW

I am here.

Name _____

Grade _____

School _____

Who I am.

Make a word collage! Use 5 adjectives to form a picture that describes who you are.

Where I'm going.

The next career pathway I want to explore is

_____

Some things I need to learn first to succeed.

1 _____

2 _____

3 _____

My Career Choice

To get here.

GLOSSARY

actuary a person who compiles and analyzes statistics and uses them to calculate insurance risks and premiums

appraisal an expert estimate of the value of a house or other type of property

budgets plans for how much money a person, family, or company will earn and spend during a particular period of time

chief financial officer person who is the senior executive responsible for managing the finances of a company

deductible specific amount of money that an insured person must pay before an insurance company will pay a claim

embezzlement the process of secretly stealing money from a place of business

ethics moral code of decent human behavior; acting in a way that is good and honest

executives people who have the highest level jobs in a company

FBI a government agency that helps protect the nation from dangerous threats; stands for Federal Bureau of Investigation

financial planner person who manages the personal finances of clients

forensic accountant person who uses accounting skills to investigate fraud or embezzlement for use in legal disputes

fraud dishonest behavior and tricks that are intended to deceive people or get money from them

insurance an arrangement in which someone pays money to a company that agrees to pay the person a certain amount in the event of sickness, fire, accident, or other property loss

insurance claims agent person who investigates insurance claims to find out how much an insurance company needs to pay for that claim

interest a fee paid for borrowing money, usually a percentage of the amount borrowed

investments money that has been put into something with the intention of getting more money back later

master of business administration a graduate degree earned at college that prepares students for careers in business management

money laundering concealing money obtained illegally by transferring it through legal businesses or banks

mortgage a loan from a bank used to buy a house or other property

mortgage broker person who works as a middleman between someone who needs a loan to buy a house and a lender who can provide the funds

purchasing agent person who purchases materials and supplies to be used by a business

risk the possibility of loss, harm, or danger

spreadsheets computer programs that allow you to keep track of and use numerical information in a table format

stock share or part ownership of a business sold to investors on the stock exchange

stockbroker person who buys and sells securities on a stock exchange on behalf of clients

stock exchange marketplace where stocks are bought and sold

stockholders people or companies that invest in stocks and own shares of a business

vendors people who sell something

white-collar crimes nonviolent crimes involving money that are committed by business or government professionals

INDEX

* Refers to the Web page sources

About the Author

Diane Lindsey Reeves is the author of lots of children's books. She has written several original PEANUTS stories (published by Regnery Kids and Sourcebooks). She is especially curious about what people do and likes to write books that get kids thinking about all the cool things they can be when they grow up. She lives in Cary, North Carolina, and her favorite thing to do is play with her grandkids—Conrad, Evan, Reid, and Hollis Grace.